POCKET
MANUAL

Scottis

D1589337

The fastest road and racing cars

WORLD'S FASTEST CARS

© Haynes Publishing 2010

Published in April 2010.
Reprinted August 2010.

British Library Cataloguing-in-Publication Data:
A catalogue record for this book is available from
the British Library

ISBN 978 1 84425 965 6

Published by Haynes Publishing,
Sparkford, Yeovil, Somerset BA22 7JJ, UK
Tel: 01963 442030 Fax: 01963 440001
Int. tel: +44 1963 442030 Int. fax: +44 1963 440001
Email: sales@haynes.co.uk
Website: www.haynes.co.uk

Haynes North America, Inc.,
861 Lawrence Drive, Newbury Park
California 91320, USA

Design and layout by Lee Parsons

All photographs courtesy www.magiccarpics.co.uk except for:
LAT; page 10, 20, 24, 25, 27

Printed in the USA

The Author

Richard Dredge got addicted to cars when he was a
child, rebuilding his first Triumph at 16. He contributes to
publications such as *Octane*, *Practical Classics* and *Auto
Express*. For a fuller CV, visit www.richarddredge.com

POCKET MANUAL

Haynes

The fastest road and racing cars on Earth

WORLD'S FASTEST CARS

CONTENTS

COMPETITION CARS 6

AERO-ENGINED SPECIALS 8

DRAG RACING 12

ENDURANCE RACING 16

FORMULA ONE 20

LAND SPEED RECORD 30

ROAD CARS 38

9FF 40

ASCARI 42

ASTON MARTIN 44

BENTLEY 48

BRABUS 52

BRISTOL 54

BUGATTI 56

CALLAWAY 58

CAPARO 60

CHEVROLET 62

CIZETA 64

DAUER 66

FERRARI 68

FORD 74

GUMPERT 76

INVICTA 78

JAGUAR 80

KEATING 82

KOENIGSEGG 84

LAMBORGHINI 86

LEXUS 92

LOTEC 94

MASERATI 96

McLAREN 98

MERCEDES 100

NOBLE 104

PAGANI 106

PORSCHE 108

SALEEN 114

SHELBY 116

SPYKER 118

ULTIMA 120

VECTOR 122

YAMAHA 124

ZENVO 126

WORLD'S FASTEST COMPETITION CARS

Racing cars are built for one reason only – to go fast. Often, money is no object, with the most high-tech engineering being used in a bid to gain those extra few miles per hour. Over the next few pages you'll be able to read about how cheap horsepower was available in the 1920s and 1930s, which resulted in some spectacular machines being created – and ones that were rolling death traps.

You can also read about how Formula One got started as well as what goes into making the fastest machines on Earth – Land Speed Record cars, which can now touch the speed of sound. However, even though the Land Speed Record is already faster than the speed of sound, there are plans to smash through the 1000mph barrier. Now *that's* fast!

AERO-ENGINED SPECIALS
THE FASTEST DEATH TRAPS EVER MADE

The problem with wanting to go seriously fast is that it needs a seriously powerful engine – and those tend to be expensive to buy as well as to run. However, during the 1920s and 1930s, there was a handy solution: surplus aircraft engines from the First World War. Available relatively cheaply, these offered far more power than road car engines of the time, and they were also reliable too.

As a result of these powerplants being widely available, a stack of aero-engined cars were created, offering massive power and speed, but usually so crudely engineered that it's amazing any of them ever survived a run without destroying themselves and their drivers.

Often driven by a chain, fitted with the most basic braking and suspension systems, and running on narrow tyres, the typical aero-engined car was a rolling death trap.

Because these cars were light and powerful, they were perfect for tackling the land speed record, and that's why several pre-war records were held by ▶

aero-engined cars. One of the most famous was 'Babs', powered by a 27-litre V12 Liberty aero engine and an evolution of the Chitty Bang Bang which later evolved into the Higham Special. At the hands of Parry Thomas, Babs claimed the land speed record in 1926, at 171.02mph on Pendine Sands in south Wales. In 1927, Thomas was attempting another record run in Babs when he was killed in a crash; there's still debate over whether a wheel collapsed or the drive chain broke and decapitated him.

Another well-known aero-engined special was the Napier-Railton, built in 1933 for John Cobb, who raced it at Brooklands. He holds the all-time speed record there, at 143.44mph, powered by a 500bhp 23,944cc W12 engine. Capable of just 5mpg, this must have been a frightening beast to drive at speed around Brooklands' concrete surface – especially as it had brakes only on the rear wheels!

The aero-engined car wasn't unique to the pre-war years though,

DID YOU KNOW? An engine produces both power and torque; usually, the bigger the engine, the more of both are produced. A car's top speed is generally governed by the available power, while its acceleration is down to the torque.

as in the 1960s, Paul Jameson installed a 27-litre Rolls-Royce Merlin engine into a self-built chassis. Before fitting a body though, the project was sold to John Dodd, who constructed an outlandish bodyshell and named the car 'The Beast'. After being destroyed in a fire, the car has been rebuilt and is still in use.

Dodd's 'The Beast'

DRAG RACING
THE MOST DRAMATIC CARS EVER BUILT

Cars come no more extreme than a top fuel dragster. Built for one reason only – to accelerate as quickly as possible – these cars represent the peak of automotive engineering. Capable of accelerating from a standstill to around 250mph in just six seconds or so over a 440-yard stretch of Tarmac, a top fuel dragster gathers speed faster than a fighter jet, or a Formula One race car.

Each cylinder produces around 1000bhp, and with a 0–100mph time of under a second, a top fuel dragster leaves the start line with a force nearly five times that of gravity, the same force as the space shuttle when it leaves the launch pad at Cape

Canaveral. But it all comes at a cost; these monsters consume 4–5 gallons of fuel during a quarter-mile run, equivalent to 16–20 gallons per mile!

Drag racing started out in the late 1940s on the dry lake beds of California's Mojave Desert; in those days all the racing was unofficial and top speeds were little more than 100mph. ▶

Vanishing Point

DID YOU KNOW?

A drag racer has so much power, that it has to be fed in gradually, using a series of slipping clutches, to stop the car from flipping over backwards.

The cars were usually street legal, but it wasn't long before properly regulated drag racing arrived, and the Santa Ana Drags in Southern California opened in 1950. By the middle of that decade the best cars were managing 140mph over the line; three decades later this speed had doubled and by 1992 the fastest cars were achieving 300mph in just a quarter of a mile. Just seven years later, the 330mph barrier was broken.

While most drag racers feature piston engines, a few have a jet engine instead. Used more for show than for serious competition, there's little to separate

DID YOU KNOW?

A drag racer's tyres start out wide and low, but become much taller and narrower at the moment the car launches off the line. This raises the gearing, allowing the car to go faster.

jet-engined and top fuel dragsters in terms of drama or performance. Both are one of the most amazing sights on Earth, both are equally fast and either of them can lead to a driver passing out from the G forces endured throughout a full-bore quarter-mile run. Drag racing is most definitely not for the faint-hearted!

KEY CAR
ANDY CARTER TOP FUEL DRAGSTER (2006)

BUILT	2006
ENGINE	8190cc, rear-mounted V8
POWER	8000bhp
TORQUE	N/A
TOP SPEED	317mph
0–60MPH	0.5sec

ENDURANCE RACING
MASSIVE SPEED WITH PHENOMENAL DURABILITY

While drag races are over in a few seconds, endurance racing lasts for hours – often 24 of them. So while this form of motorsport is still very much about performance, it's also about reliability; sitting at 150mph+ for hour after hour requires some very special engineering if the cars are to survive. Endurance races aren't always run over a fixed time though; sometimes it's the distance that's fixed, usually at 1000km, or 620 miles.

The first endurance race was held at Brooklands in 1907; it lasted 24 hours. However, the most famous and prestigious endurance race of them all is the Le Mans 24 Hours, which has run annually since 1923. It's not the only race of its type though, as the 24 Hours of Daytona is an American equivalent while there's also the 12 Hours of Sebring, also in the US.

Endurance racing takes a lot of stamina on the part of the drivers, while in one race, the car has to withstand the same sort of wear and tear that a Formula One car will endure in a whole season – with a rebuild between each race. Because the cars are built to last, their engines can't be too highly stressed, or reliability would suffer. The typical power output for a Le Mans car

is only 600–700bhp; by the mid-1930s, some Le Mans cars were already generating over 300bhp, so power outputs haven't increased by as much as you might think.

In recent years the most successful cars have been diesel-powered, with Audi and Peugeot battling it out between them. By far the most frequent winner

of the Le Mans 24 Hours has been Porsche, which has taken gold on 16 occasions, including six consecutive wins between 1981 and 1987. A string of iconic cars such as the 917, 956 and 962 enabled Porsche to claim one victory after another – but now it looks as though Audi's domination is set to continue, with the odd break.

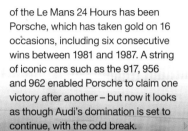

KEY CAR
PORSCHE 962

BUILT	1984
ENGINE	2869cc, mid-mounted turbocharged flat-six
POWER	680bhp @ 8200rpm
TORQUE	486lb ft @ 5800rpm
TOP SPEED	225mph approx
0–60MPH	N/A

Bentley Speed 8

DID YOU KNOW? The 1923 Le Mans 24 Hour winners averaged 57.5mph over 1380 miles. The 2009 event winners averaged 135mph over 3259 miles.

KEY CAR
AUDI R10 TDI

BUILT	2006
ENGINE	5500cc, mid-mounted turbocharged V12
POWER	650bhp
TORQUE	811lb ft
TOP SPEED	230mph approx
0–60MPH	N/A

FORMULA ONE
THE PINNACLE OF AUTOMOTIVE ENGINEERING

The premier league of motorsport has long been seen as Formula One, partly because of the massive budgets and the glamour, but largely because of the astonishing level of engineering that goes into each car. Formula One is directly descended from Grand Prix racing, which began in France in 1894. Organised by Parisian newspaper *Le Petit Journal*, this first Grand Prix was run over 80 miles of public roads. However, the term 'Grand Prix' (Grand Prize) wasn't properly used in racing until the 1901 Grand Prix de Pau.

Over the following years there would be a series of Grands Prix, all on public roads and each leaving a trail of

Brawn GP – 2009

Renault Type K

carnage and chaos behind them. The turning point came in 1903, when many drivers and pedestrians were killed during the Paris–Madrid road race, which was stopped because of the high casualty rate; further road-based racing was banned as a result.

After 1903, races were run on closed public roads, such as those around Le Mans, where from 1906 there were regular Grands Prix on a 65-mile triangular circuit. Just a year later, though, the world's first purpose-built racing circuit was built, at Brooklands in Surrey, England. Two years later came Indianapolis in the US and by 1922, Monza's national autodrome had also been completed.

During the 1920s and 1930s things became more tightly regulated and better organised. However, a major change came when the FIA (Federation Internationale de l'Automobile), set up in 1947, organised the first Formula One race, ▶

Auto Union Type C

DID YOU KNOW?

Transmissions have developed massively thanks to Formula One. The biggest stride has been in sequential gearboxes, operated by paddle shifts, which allow gears to be swapped in two hundredths of a second.

which was run at Silverstone in 1950. That first event was won by Giuseppe Farina in an Alfa Romeo; it was this Italian marque which dominated the first year of Formula One. However, also on the grid was Ferrari, which has stuck with Formula One from its earliest days right through to the present day – the only entrant to do so.

Those early races saw a mixture of car types competing, some featuring supercharged 1.5-litre engines and others being fitted with normally aspirated (not supercharged or turbocharged) 4.5-litre powerplants. The winning Alfas featured the former while Ferrari decided to take the latter route, due to the ferocious thirst of the

supercharged 1.5-litre engine. When opened up, these engines burned fuel at the rate of around 2mpg, which actually slowed the cars down because of the number of fuel stops they had to make.

The 1950s saw the arrival of a string of racing cars that went on to become truly iconic. Alfa Romeo's 158 'Alfetta' dominated the first season of Formula

KEY CAR
MASERATI 250F

BUILT	1954
ENGINE	2494cc, front-mounted straight-six
POWER	270bhp @ 8000rpm
TORQUE	N/A
TOP SPEED	155mph
0–60MPH	N/A

DID YOU KNOW? In the 1950s and 1960s, most F1 cars had just 200–220bhp, but by the mid-1980s many were producing 1300bhp or more. By the late 1980s, power had dropped to 700bhp or so, where they've remained.

Mercedes W196

One (it took all three of the first places for the year) while Ferrari's 500 of 1952/3 won every race it entered except one. Mercedes also caused a stir when it returned to Formula One in 1954, with its straight-eight W196, which won three-quarters of the races it entered.

By 1958, every Formula One car ever built was rendered obsolete overnight, ▷

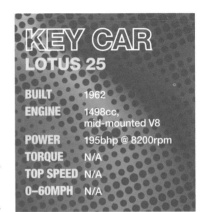

DID YOU KNOW?

A normal road car engine revs to around 7000rpm, but a Formula One engine typically revs to 20,000rpm. F1 cars no longer have turbochargers, but many road cars do; these turbos typically rev at 150,000rpm.

by the arrival of Cooper's T43, which won the Argentine Grand Prix that year. This was truly a landmark car, as it was the first in Formula One to have the engine behind the driver rather than in front – although other Grand Prix cars, such as Auto Union's C and D-Type of the 1930s, used a similar layout. It was clear that Cooper was onto a winner with the T43 because within a year the car had been developed into the T51, which Jack Brabham then used to win the 1959 and 1960 drivers' titles. The car was so good that there were nine of them on the grid of the 1960 British Grand Prix, entered by six teams.

The next big step was the

Lotus 49

adoption of monocoque construction, by Lotus for its Type 49 in 1963. Actually it was little more than a tub flanked by pontoons for the fuel tanks, but at least it wasn't a tubular steel frame covered in body panels, like all single-seaters so far. By 1967 there was another big step with the launch of the Ford Cosworth DFV ▷

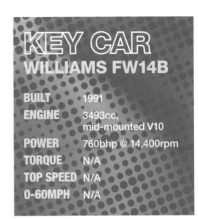

 **DID YOU KNOW?** In 1976, Tyrrell unveiled an F1 car, the P34, with four front wheels, the idea being that because there were two pairs, they could be reduced in diameter to reduce drag. The idea didn't catch on.

engine; this was the most successful powerplant in Formula One history as it kept notching up wins right through to 1985.

When the six-wheeled Tyrrell P34 arrived in 1976, many felt this was the way forward, but it proved a blind alley. What wasn't, was turbocharging, introduced by Renault in 1977. Reliability issues meant there were no victories until 1979, but by this point everyone was using turbocharging, which remained popular until it was banned in 1988.

Throughout the 1980s and 1990s there were many more technical innovations, including electronic management and telemetry systems, carbon-fibre construction and active suspension, along with semi-automatic gearboxes, allowing a greater number of gears for the driver. There are many who feel that massive budgets and ever more sophisticated cars have reduced spectator excitement as well as driver skills, but what can't be denied is that road cars continue to benefit from technology developed on the circuit, ensuring we all benefit in the end.

KEY CAR
FERRARI F2004

BUILT	2004
ENGINE	2997cc, mid-mounted V10
POWER	900bhp approx
TORQUE	N/A
TOP SPEED	230mph approx
0–60MPH	1.8sec approx

DID YOU KNOW?

The modern Formula One car's brake discs can reach 1000°C under hard braking; they can allow the car to accelerate from 0 to 100mph and back to zero in just five seconds.

LAND SPEED RECORD
THE FASTEST OF THE FASTEST

When it comes to pushing the boundaries, nothing can compare with a land speed record car. These represent the absolute peak of technology in terms of aerodynamics, engine technology, braking and construction. While everything is now developed on computer, it wasn't always so – many of the early land speed record cars were crudely engineered tubs on wheels, with a surplus aeroplane engine squeezed in.

The first record-breaking cars weren't so frightening, however; the first six records held were all by electric cars, starting at 39.24mph in December 1898 and rising steadily to 65.79mph over the next 18 months, when a steam-driven Gardner-Serpollet clocked up 75.06mph in 1902. When a Mors driven by American William Vanderbilt then claimed the record just a few months later, at 76.08mph, it marked the beginning of a domination by piston-engined cars (aside from a Stanley steam-powered record in

Bluebird 2

1906), which lasted until 1963, when jet and rocket-engined cars took over.

Most famous of the wheel-driven record breakers was Malcolm Campbell, who famously ran a series of cars called Bluebird. Campbell first broke the record in 1924, at 146mph; by 1935 he'd taken this to 301mph – the first man on Earth to break the 300mph barrier.

Such speeds would seem positively slow by the 1960s though, when jet engines started to be used. First was Craig Breedlove with Spirit of America, ▶

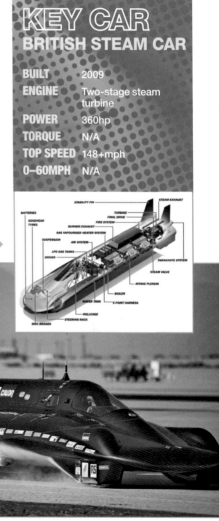

KEY CAR
BRITISH STEAM CAR

BUILT	2009
ENGINE	Two-stage steam turbine
POWER	360hp
TORQUE	N/A
TOP SPEED	148+mph
0–60MPH	N/A

then Thrust SSC to 763mph in 1997 – claiming the first supersonic land speed record in the process.

As this book was written, the ultimate land speed record contender was unveiled: Richard Noble's Bloodhound SSC. Demonstrating just how high the stakes are at this level, Bloodhound went through no fewer than 10 redesigns in 27 months to get the layout and details right. With a jet engine as well as a rocket producing 33,150bhp between them, and a target top speed of 1000mph, the consequences of getting the slightest detail wrong are nothing short of alarming...

which ran at 408mph – within two years Breedlove achieved almost 601mph in Spirit of America – Sonic 1. From this point on, the bar was raised in smaller steps; in 1983, Andy Green took Thrust 2 to 633mph and

OTHER SPEED RECORDS

It's not just the absolute speed record that tempts record breakers; there are all sorts of others too. One is the blind speed record, which has been broken numerous times since the early 1990s. While the driver doesn't have to be blind (a blindfold can be used), everybody who has broken the record in recent ▶

years has been. In 2005, South African Hein Wagner claimed the blind speed record at just over 151mph in a Maserati Coupé; three years later this was raised to 182mph by Belgian Luc Costermans in a Lamborghini Gallardo.

In the meantime, also in 2005, Brit Mike Newman had taken the record to 178.5mph in a derestricted BMW M5. He's perhaps the best known of the blind record holders, as he'd already bagged the record in 2003, at 144.7mph in a Jaguar XJR – although he'd started out on just two wheels, claiming an 89mph top speed on a motorbike. As this book went to press, he was waiting to revisit the record once more, using a Keating TKR – which you can read more about later in the book. For more on the blind speed record, take a look at www.speedofsight.co.uk

There's also the steam record, set by Fred Marriott in 1906 at 127.659mph and untouched until the British Steam Car team raised the bar to 139.8mph in 2009, driven by Don Wales. Powered by a two-stage steam turbine, the car touched 148mph but averaged just under 140mph in the timed two-way runs. More impressive is the 350.092mph by the JCB Dieselmax, in 2006, which took the record for the fastest ever diesel-engined vehicle. Driven by Andy Green (of Thrust SSC fame), the car smashed the previous 236mph record, set 35 years earlier.

Perhaps the most bizarre record is

DID YOU KNOW?

JCB Dieselmax had to be pushed by a JCB Fastrac tractor up to about 40mph before driver Andy Green could select first gear and allow the car to accelerate under its own power.

for the fastest lawnmower. It all came about after Steve Vokins, of the National Motor Museum in the UK, saw a video clip of American Bob Cleveland setting the lawnmower record at the Bonneville Salt Flats in 2006. He set the bar at 80.792mph; when Vokins saw the clip he realised that 100mph must be possible. As this book went to press the project was just being launched; to find out if the record was achieved, log on to www.projectrunningblade.co.uk

MANUAL

While a car driven by electricity would now have no hope of ever claiming the outright land speed record, in the early days, it was volts that ruled. However, even though the outright record is out of reach, that hasn't stopped teams from trying to break the existing electric records, the most recent one being Ohio State University's (OSU) Buckeye Bullet 1, which managed just under 315mph in 2004 – although the international record was set at 271mph.

Following on from the success of the electric record being claimed, the OSU decided to set the world's first fuel cell record, using Buckeye Bullet 2. Running at the Bonneville Salt Flats in September 2009, the car achieved an unofficial top speed of 303mph – to follow the team's progress, check out www.buckeyebullet.com

KEY CAR
BUCKEYE BULLET 2

BUILT	2009
ENGINE	Hydrogen fuel cell
POWER	700bhp+
TORQUE	N/A
TOP SPEED	303mph+
0–60MPH	N/A

WORLD'S FASTEST ROAD CARS

As soon as the first car turned a wheel there was a desire to go ever faster, and as long as there are those who can afford such vehicles, performance will continue to increase. Over the coming pages you can read about how companies such as Mercedes have been at the forefront of ultra-fast cars for over a century, as well as how iconic car maker Ferrari has taken its know-how gained on the track to create ever-better road cars.

Perhaps the most intriguing seriously fast cars, though, are those developed by companies with little or no background in car manufacture – never mind ultra-quick ones. Within a few short years, companies such as Spyker, Pagani and Koenigsegg came from nowhere to beat those from Italy and Germany. As this book was being written, even newer companies were coming up with fresh machinery even faster. With the fastest of those machines knocking on the door of 300mph, where will it all end?

9FF
FOR WHEN 600BHP JUST ISN'T ENOUGH

This book could have been filled with the products of tuning companies, but instead the focus has been on more mainstream production cars. However, occasionally somebody comes along with a modded car that just has to be included, because it's nothing less than barking mad. Welcome to the world of 9ff.

If you're into go-faster Porsches, you'll know all about Ruf and its products. They're completely mad and more than enough for any sane person; not Jan Fatthauer though, who left Ruf to set up his Porsche tuning outfit, 9ff, in 2001. While 9ff is happy to create breathed-on Panameras, Cayennes and even Carrera GTs, its wildest creations are all based on various versions of the 911.

The wildest car in 9ff's extensive (and expensive) line up is the GT9-R, limited to a run of 20 and successor to the GT9. Even the GT9 could manage 254mph thanks to a 987bhp 4-litre flat-six, but the GT9-R trumps even that following a power boost to 1105bhp. This gives the car a claimed top speed of 259mph, although any customers who are also wimps can opt for 750bhp or 987bhp packages. Intriguingly, 9ff does more than just tune the GT9-R's engine; it also moves it forward to create a mid-engined 911. Whatever next?

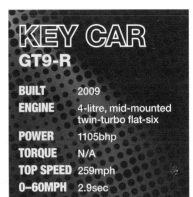

KEY CAR
GT9-R

BUILT	2009
ENGINE	4-litre, mid-mounted twin-turbo flat-six
POWER	1105bhp
TORQUE	N/A
TOP SPEED	259mph
0–60MPH	2.9sec

ASCARI
BRITAIN'S UNKNOWN SUPERCAR

Ascari first appeared in 1995, with a concept called the FGT, powered by a Chevrolet six-litre V8 and designed for track use. It looked great, but unfortunately the car proved to be far from competitive, so it was followed by the Ecosse in 1998. Once again the car looked good, but it proved very hard to sell because no one had really heard of Ascari.

After just 17 Ecosses had been built, it was followed by the KZ-1, which was a far more grown-up machine – but so was its price tag. Costing three times as much as a Porsche 911, the KZ-1 was fast and beautifully built but very costly.

That didn't worry company founder Klaas Zwart, who announced that only 50 examples would be built.

The KZ-1 was powered by a 5-litre BMW V8, taken from the M5 and breathed on to produce a very handy 500bhp. Weight was kept to a minimum using a carbon-fibre bodyshell, and with its mid-engined configuration the KZ-1 certainly proved nimble; the race-spec KZ-1R was even more agile. However, compared with more mainstream rivals, most who drove the Ascari thought it wasn't worth the extra cash, which is why it has always maintained a low profile.

KEY CAR
ASCARI KZ-1

BUILT	2000
ENGINE	4941cc, mid-mounted V8
POWER	500bhp @ 7000rpm
TORQUE	368lb ft @ 4500rpm
TOP SPEED	200mph
0–60MPH	3.8sec

ASTON MARTIN
THE GENTLEMAN'S SUPERCAR

Despite passing through one owner after another since the company was founded in 1913, Aston Martin has come up with some of the most elegant sportscars ever made. Numerous high points include a string of pre-war road racers as well as the DB5 of 1963 and the 1977 V8 Vantage, which would give way to the Virage of

1989 – which in turn would ultimately be developed into the 600bhp Vantage V600 Coupé in 1998.

Founded by Lionel Martin and Robert Bamford, Aston Martin moved premises and changed hands numerous times, until in 1947 it was bought by David Brown, along with another luxury marque; Lagonda. Three years later,

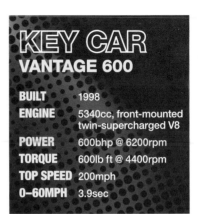

BUILT	1998
ENGINE	5340cc, front-mounted twin-supercharged V8
POWER	600bhp @ 6200rpm
TORQUE	600lb ft @ 4400rpm
TOP SPEED	200mph
0–60MPH	3.9sec

the first DB-badged Aston Martin was introduced: the DB1, followed by the DB3 racer in 1957. The DB4 of 1958 was a new direction for Aston Martin, as its design was much more modern, but its 145mph DB5 successor of 1963 proved to be a real turning point for the company, as it featured heavily in cult James Bond film *Goldfinger*, alongside Sean Connery, thrusting this small British company well and truly into the limelight.

It was all change for 1967, with the Williams Towns-designed DBS, which used DB6 mechanicals in a completely new bodyshell. However, by 1969 the six-cylinder engine had been superseded by a 5340cc V8, which then powered all Aston Martins until the 335bhp DB7 of 1994. This DB7 was initially powered by a supercharged straight-six, but the 435bhp V12-engined DB7 Vantage of 1999 was far more appealing – and so was the even more capable Vanquish that arrived two years later and could achieve 196mph.

The DB7 – and all the models that followed it – had come about thanks to the purchase of Aston Martin by Ford in 1987. Until this point, the company struggled to make cars profitably. However, Ford's purchase of the company meant an all-new factory ▶

KEY CAR
DBS

BUILT	2008
ENGINE	5935cc, V12
POWER	510bhp @ 6500rpm
TORQUE	420lb ft @ 5750rpm
TOP SPEED	194mph
0–60MPH	4.2sec

and much higher production volumes, allowing quality to improve while also putting the company on a far better financial footing.

Although Ford sold Aston Martin in 2007, while it was responsible for the company's product development it invested heavily in new production facilities and new construction techniques. As a direct result of this, Aston Martin was able to produce one great car after another, including the 190mph DB9 of 2003, the V8 Vantage of 2005 and the DBS of 2008, the latter model replacing the DBS and introduced under its new owners.

BENTLEY
THE MOST ELEGANT SUPERCARS EVER BUILT

The 4½-Litre Blower Bentley was known as 'the fastest lorry in the world' when it arrived in 1929, and for good reason. It was massive and with a 100mph top speed it was astonishingly fast for its day, but at that speed it burned fuel at the rate of 2.8mpg!

Bentley had started production in 1919, but by 1931 it had gone bust and been swallowed up by Rolls-Royce. As a result, the two companies' models were developed side by side after the mid-1930s. However, Bentleys were still seen as the sporting option, which is why there was no Rolls-Royce equivalent to the R-Type Continental which arrived in 1952. Billed as the fastest four-seater in the world and fitted with a 4566cc straight-

Bentley R-Type

six, it was capable of 115mph at a time when most family saloons struggled to reach 70mph. Unsurprisingly, the R-Type Continental was very expensive, which is why just 165 cars were built during a seven-year production run.

The R-Type Continental would be the last Bentley without a Rolls-Royce equivalent, until the Continental R ▶

Bentley R-Type Continental

HSU 586

arrived in 1991. Along the way there were the S-Series, T-Series and Mulsanne, the latter including a range of derivatives such as the Brooklands, Eight and Turbo R.

The next turning point came in 2003, with the unveiling of the Continental GT, after Bentley was bought by the Volkswagen Group in 1998. The Continental GT was the first all-new car from Bentley in more than half a century; in standard form, as first released, it was capable of 198mph, thanks to a 5998cc W12 engine. However, the model went on to be developed into the Flying Spur saloon, the GTC convertible and then the amazingly quick Speed model. In this latter form the car was capable of a genuine 202mph after fitting a 602bhp W12 engine in the nose. However, even this was beaten by the Supersports edition that followed, with its 204mph top speed.

Incidentally, Bentley has only ever built front-engined cars for sale, but in 1999 it created the Hunaudières concept; a mid-engined supercar fitted with a 623bhp 8-litre W16. Using the same engine that eventually powered the Bugatti Veyron, the Hunaudières proved to be a one-off, as the VW Group had enough supercar development on its hands with the Veyron, the Audi R8 and Lamborghini's Gallardo as well as the Murciélago.

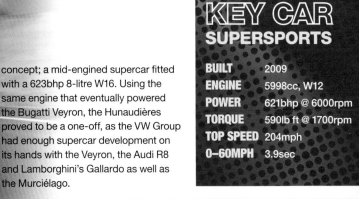

KEY CAR
SUPERSPORTS

BUILT	2009
ENGINE	5998cc, W12
POWER	621bhp @ 6000rpm
TORQUE	590lb ft @ 1700rpm
TOP SPEED	204mph
0–60MPH	3.9sec

BRABUS
200MPH TRANSPORT FOR FOUR

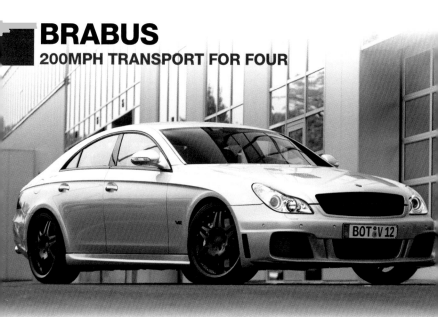

Brabus was started way back in 1977, by Klaus Brackmann and Bodo Buschmann; the company took its name from the first three letters of each founder's name. Ever since it set up shop, Brabus has focused on creating some of the fastest and most luxurious Mercedes-Benzes ever made. No matter what the car's size, there's always room for a bored-out V8 or V12 under the bonnet.

Perhaps best known for its (relatively) fast Smarts, Brabus also offers tuned versions of every car in the Mercedes line up, from the A-Class right through to the Maybach, with the Viano van along the way. Choosing the maddest product is hard when there are so many utterly insane cars on offer, but the two highlights are probably the Bullitt and the Rocket.

The Bullitt is based on the third-generation C-Class, and a 730bhp 6233cc twin-turbo V12 is squeezed under the bonnet to give a 224mph top speed, which should be enough for most buyers. However, if this isn't quite quick enough, there's always the CLS-based Rocket. This uses the same V12 but, because of the CLS's better aerodynamics, it has a top speed of 228mph. Well, you never know when you might need those few extra miles per hour…

KEY CAR
ROCKET

BUILT	2006
ENGINE	6233cc, front-mounted twin-turbo V12
POWER	730bhp @ 5100rpm
TORQUE	811lb ft @ 2100rpm
TOP SPEED	228mph
0–60MPH	4.0sec

BRISTOL
THE ORIGINAL GENTLEMAN'S EXPRESS

Bristol has never felt the need to conform; it's one of those companies that does things its own way, for a very select number of connoisseurs. Founded in 1945 and directly descended from the Bristol Aeroplane Company, Bristol Cars has only ever made a tiny number of cars each year, each one lovingly crafted by hand.

Always featuring distinctive styling and fitted with unstressed, powerful engines, nowhere is the Bristol philosophy more apparent than with the Fighter. With its gull-wing doors, narrow bodyshell and Chrysler Viper V10 engine in the nose, there really is nothing else like it.

Even the standard Fighter can top 210mph, with its 525bhp, but for those who feel that too much power is not enough, the Fighter T was unveiled in 2007. With a claimed 1012bhp, the car can theoretically manage 270mph – but it's electronically limited to a 'more than sufficient' 225mph.

While the top speed is only claimed – and not proved – if it is possible then it's largely down to the ultra-slippery bodyshell rather than a low kerb weight. With a drag co-efficient of just 0.28, the Fighter is more aerodymanic than most of its rivals, but it also has a heavy steel chassis – no high-tech carbon-fibre here.

KEY CAR
FIGHTER T

BUILT	2007
ENGINE	7996cc, front-mounted V10
POWER	1012bhp @ 5600rpm
TORQUE	1036lb ft @ 4500rpm
TOP SPEED	225mph
0–60MPH	3.5sec

BUGATTI
NOT THE WORLD'S FASTEST PRODUCTION CAR...

In the pre-war years, Bugatti produced some of the most desirable sporting machines ever created, but the marque only just survived into the post-war years. In the mid-1980s the brand was revived though, to create the crazy EB110, so named because it was unveiled on the 110th anniversary of what would have been company founder Ettore Bugatti's birthday.

The EB110 packed in the tech and was phenomenally fast; with its quad-turbo 3.5-litre V12 it could reach 214mph. But the car was also hugely expensive to build, which is why Bugatti went bust after just 115 had been built.

Thankfully the story doesn't end there though, as the Volkswagen Group resurrected Bugatti and launched a car that would be even faster than the mighty McLaren F1 – the Veyron. With its quad-turbo W16 engine and four-wheel drive, the Veyron was extremely complicated, which is why it took years to develop. The car would have bankrupted a smaller company, but Volkswagen stuck with it and revealed the Veyron to the world in 2005 – at 252mph it immediately became the world's fastest car. Unfortunately for Bugatti though, it wouldn't take long for a faster production car to come along…

KEY CAR
VEYRON

BUILT	2005
ENGINE	7993cc, mid-mounted quad-turbo W16
POWER	987bhp
TORQUE	922lb ft
TOP SPEED	252mph
0–60MPH	3.0sec

CALLAWAY

Reeves Callaway set up shop in 1977, offering turbocharger kits for BMW, Audi, Porsche and Mercedes cars. But it would be another decade before Callaway's first tuned Corvette would be available. Known as the C4, and available as an official factory product through Corvette dealers, over 500 such cars were produced. On offer was a twin-turbo conversion, with the ultimate edition being the Sledgehammer, which until 1999 was officially the world's fastest production car, with a 254.76mph top speed.

Before the Sledgehammer was killed off, the Corvette-based C12 made its debut, in 1997. Created to win the GT2 class at Le Mans, road and race variants were developed side by side, with 20 cars built in all. With a 5666cc V8 there was 440bhp on tap, which was enough to propel the C12 to 190mph. Beautifully designed and homologated for road use as a Callaway rather than a Corvette, the C12 would prove to be a major milestone for the company.

Callaway took another leap forward in 2006, with the unveiling of its C16. Offered in manual or automatic forms (with 216 and 205mph top speeds respectively), the C16 was also offered with a choice of three bodystyles: coupé, convertible or speedster, the latter supplied complete with aeroscreens, fairings and the most gorgeous detailing.

KEY CAR
C16

BUILT	2006
ENGINE	6.2 litres, front-mounted supercharged V8
POWER	616bhp @ 6200rpm
TORQUE	582lb ft @ 4750rpm
TOP SPEED	216mph
0–60MPH	3.3sec

CAPARO
THE MOST EXTREME HYPERCAR YET

Early in 2006, the covers were taken off what was possibly the most extreme-looking road car ever created, up to that point. The Freestream T1 looked like a cross between an insect and a full-race single-seater. With a power-to-weight ratio of around 1000bhp per tonne, it was able to upset some of the existing supercar elite.

The T1 was the brainchild of ex-McLaren staff Ben Scott-Geddes and Graham Halstead, who had worked on the iconic F1. However, before the T1 had the chance to go into limited production under the Freestream name, the project was snapped up by American company Caparo Vehicle Technologies.

When Caparo took over the project, the proposed powerplant was a supercharged 2.4-litre V8, capable of delivering 480bhp at 10,500rpm. That's clearly a handy amount of power, particularly when you consider the T1's kerb weight was just 465kg, due to the extensive use of high-tech composites and aluminium. However, by the time the T1 was unveiled in production form, the all-alloy engine had grown to 3.5 litres and power had been boosted to 575bhp. For serious track-day enthusiasts, even this wasn't enough though, which is why in 2009 a 620bhp version was unveiled, capable of 0–100mph in just 5.8 seconds.

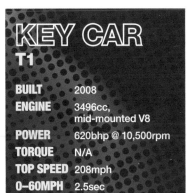

KEY CAR
T1

BUILT	2008
ENGINE	3496cc, mid-mounted V8
POWER	620bhp @ 10,500rpm
TORQUE	N/A
TOP SPEED	208mph
0–60MPH	2.5sec

CHEVROLET
AMERICA'S HOME-GROWN SUPERCAR GROWS UP

Ever since the Corvette was launched in 1953, it has defined the American supercar. While those early editions weren't especially fast, as time progressed the Corvette got ever more powerful and faster. The first high point came with the 1967 Sting Ray, which packed a 430bhp 7-litre V8; two years later the 550bhp ZL-1 option hit the streets. This would prove to be the ultimate – at least in terms of available power – until the ZR-1 arrived in 2009.

The 2009 ZR-1 was based on the sixth-generation Corvette and it was the most powerful factory-built production Corvette ever. The ZR-1 tag had been used before, though, in a Lotus-tuned version of the fourth-generation Corvette – but that was positively lame in comparison. That first model had packed just 375bhp (later 405bhp) – but from the outset the newer model could offer 638bhp and 604lb ft of torque from its supercharged 6.2-litre V8.

This level of power meant the LS9 V8 of the ZR-1 was the most powerful engine ever fitted to a General Motors car. It was also enough to give a top speed of 205mph, and things were helped enormously by the fitment of lightweight carbon-fibre panels, including the wings, roof, bonnet and various interior trim mouldings.

KEY CAR
CORVETTE ZR-1

BUILT	2009
ENGINE	6162cc, front-mounted supercharged V8
POWER	638bhp @ 6500rpm
TORQUE	604lb ft @ 3800rpm
TOP SPEED	205mph
0–60MPH	3.5sec

CIZETA
THE CRAZIEST SUPERCAR EVER

If supercars are about extremes, this must be the ultimate, thanks to a crazy 5995cc 16-cylinder engine – transversely mounted! No wonder the Cizeta was so wide; it had eight cylinders across its girth. With 560bhp at a dizzying 8000rpm, the noise was awe-inspiring, with 64 valves all doing their stuff.

The outrageous Cizeta came about during the supercar boom of the 1980s; buyers couldn't get enough of them, which is why a stack of new models were developed. This one was designed by Marcello Gandini, who also penned the Lamborghini Countach – no wonder the two cars looked so similar. Financing the project was musician Giorgio Moroder and businessman Claudio Zampolli, whose initials (CZ) were used for the car's name – CZ is pronounced 'chee-zeta' in Italian.

With such an impressive powerplant in the middle, it was claimed the V16T could top 204mph, but nobody ever officially tested the car, so who knows? Despite the prototype emerging in 1989, it was 1992 before the first cars were ready. In the meantime, money man Giorgio Moroder walked away, but the car lingered on until 1995. In all, just nine coupés were built, but in 2005 a further four roadsters were made.

KEY CAR
V16T

BUILT	1991
ENGINE	5995cc, mid-mounted V16
POWER	560bhp @ 8000rpm
TORQUE	469lb ft @ 6000rpm
TOP SPEED	204mph
0–60MPH	4.4sec

DAUER
A LE MANS RACER FOR THE ROAD

The 1990s was a great decade for Porsche 962 fans, thanks to a flurry of road-going supercars inspired by Porsche's brilliant endurance racer. Among them was Vern Schuppan's homage to the 962, while there were also the Koenig C62 and the DP962 from DP Motorsports. However, the best of them all was the Dauer 962 Le Mans, created by ex-racer and team owner Jochen Dauer.

The basis for Dauer's 962 Le Mans was a genuine Porsche 962 chassis, stripped down, upgraded, then wrapped in a high-tech carbon-fibre bodyshell. In the process, Dauer also took the chance to improve the aerodynamics, fitting a more streamlined undertray while he was at it. Because the factory racers were fitted with just the one seat, another was added to turn the Le Mans into a two-seater.

KEY CAR
962 LE MANS

BUILT	1993
ENGINE	2994cc, mid-mounted twin-turbo flat-six
POWER	730bhp @ 7400rpm
TORQUE	517lb ft @ 5000rpm
TOP SPEED	238mph
0–60MPH	2.8sec

Mechanically, the car was much the same as the 962s that raced at Le Mans, with a 3-litre engine. However, because Dauer's road car didn't have to comply with racing regulations, it produced a very useful 730bhp – enough to give a 238mph claimed top speed. The car arrived at the 1993 Frankfurt motor show, with a price tag of over £150,000. As a result, just a dozen or so cars were built.

FERRARI
THE WORLD'S MOST GLAMOROUS SUPERCARS

Has any car maker ever been more revered than Ferrari? Thanks to massive Formula One success, this truly iconic Italian car maker captures the imagination like no other supercar builder could ever do. There have been so many Ferrari high spots since the company was formed in 1947 that it's hard to pick out individual cars.

The 250GTO of 1962 was undoubtedly a landmark for Ferrari though, as it was a racer homologated for road use. With its 3-litre V12 there was 295bhp on tap, which was enough to take the car to 185mph – unfeasibly fast for the early 1960s.

Just 39 examples of the 250GTO were built, but by the end of the 1960s Ferrari hit another high with the 174mph 365GTB/4, nicknamed the Daytona and also powered by a V12 engine at the front. Even this seemed tame, though, compared with Ferrari's first mid-engined supercar, the Boxer. This started out as the 365BB and became the 512BB in 1976, when its flat-12 engine's capacity was increased

from 4390cc to 4942cc; with the larger engine, the car could supposedly achieve 188mph.

Following on from the Boxer was the Testarossa, which arrived in 1984. Featuring an all-new 12-cylinder boxer engine, there was 390bhp available to give a 180mph top speed. The model would be further developed in 1991 to ▶

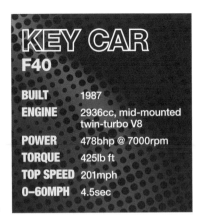

KEY CAR
F40

BUILT	1987
ENGINE	2936cc, mid-mounted twin-turbo V8
POWER	478bhp @ 7000rpm
TORQUE	425lb ft
TOP SPEED	201mph
0–60MPH	4.5sec

become the 512TR; four years later it evolved into the 196mph F512M.

Arguably, Ferrari's all-time peak was reached with the debut of the F40 in 1987, which was built to celebrate 40 years of the company's existence. This wasn't a milestone because of its amazing technology; it shone because of a lack of gadgetry, which allowed the driver to get on with enjoying every mile. The F40 was descended from the 189mph 288GTO of 1984, which started life as a track car. When Ferrari turned it into a road car, every example it could make was sold instantly; there was clearly a ready market for seriously focused driver's cars that did little to mollycoddle its occupants.

The keys to the F40's phenomenal abilities were its low weight and massive power; it weighed just 1102kg due to its carbon-fibre and kevlar bodyshell, and produced 478bhp from its GTO-derived twin-turbo V8. However, this car wasn't just about outright speed as Ferrari went to great trouble to ensure it was perfectly balanced too.

The problem for Ferrari was that the F40 was so good, it would be a very tough car to beat. So when the F50 arrived a decade later to celebrate

Ferrari's 50th birthday, it was something of a let down. However, the next hypercar from Modena would make up for any disappointment in the F50; the Enzo would show that Ferrari had still got what it took to create a machine that nobody could touch.

Unofficially known as the F60, the Enzo arrived in 2002 and packed in ▸

the tech like no road car had ever done before. Designed to create increasing amounts of downforce as the speed rose, the Enzo's construction was of carbon-fibre and aluminium honeycomb throughout. Instead of a V10 there was an all-new 6-litre V12, which revved to 8200rpm, while braking was taken care of by carbon-ceramic discs.

Just 350 Enzos were built, along with 20 race editions called the FXX. Unsuitable for road use, they were offered to wealthy customers wanting a track-day toy. With an 800bhp 6.3-litre engine, this really was the ultimate supercar at the time.

The most recent V12 Ferrari has also proved to be a true great, as the

KEY CAR
599GTB

599GTB ranks easily as the most driveable 12-cylinder car it's ever built despite its amazing dynamics. The thing is, Ferrari has proved that a V12 is unnecessary; its V8-powered 458 Italia can manage 202mph and 0–62mph in 3.4 seconds, while achieving better fuel economy than any 12-cylinder engine.

BUILT	2006
ENGINE	5999cc, V12
POWER	611bhp @ 7600rpm
TORQUE	448lb ft @ 5600rpm
TOP SPEED	205mph
0–60MPH	3.7sec

FORD
THE FORD THAT BEAT FERRARI

The GT40 was designed purely to beat Ferrari at Le Mans, after Ford was beaten by Fiat to buy the Italian icon. Furious, in retaliation Ford created a supercar that was engineered in Britain but powered by an American V8. The start point was a Lola V8-powered prototype which retired from the 1963 Le Mans 24 Hours. It may have failed first time round, but the project's steel monocoque structure was reused, wrapped in glassfibre panels and went on to become a winner.

Initially known as the GT, the '40' was added because the car's roof was just 40 inches off the ground. Early cars featured a 4.2-litre V8, which was quickly upgraded to a 4.7-litre unit for more power and torque. The result was a monster that could top 200mph in race form – which is why the GT40 did indeed win the Le Mans 24 Hours, no fewer than four times.

Nearly 40 years after the arrival of the GT40, Ford decided to dust down the designs and update them, to produce an edition for the 21st century – the GT. Unveiled in 2002, the GT had a supercharged 5.4-litre V8 that offered 550bhp and a crazy 500lb ft of torque – enough to power the car to a 205mph top speed.

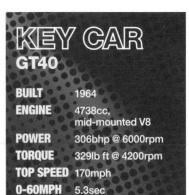

KEY CAR
GT40

BUILT	1964
ENGINE	4738cc, mid-mounted V8
POWER	306bhp @ 6000rpm
TORQUE	329lb ft @ 4200rpm
TOP SPEED	170mph
0-60MPH	5.3sec

GUMPERT
THE UNKNOWN GERMAN SUPERCAR

Turn up at the pub twirling your Gumpert key ring, and the chances are you'll be be surrounded by blank faces. That's because not only is Gumpert almost entirely unknown, but it's possibly the least glamorous-sounding car name ever devised.

The Gumpert supercar company takes its name from founder Roland Gumpert, who teamed up with Roland Mayer to create the Apollo. It was planned from the outset to be a road car that could be used on a track – with either environment allowing the car to shine. When the Apollo idea was hatched, Gumpert was working for Audi, so unsurprisingly it was that

company which provided the basis for the Apollo's motive power.

The engine chosen was Audi's V8 petrol unit, with a pair of turbos added to cook up anywhere between 641bhp and 789bhp, depending on the depth of the customer's pockets and how brave they were. If they were ecologically aware, Gumpert customers could even buy a hybrid Apollo; while this wasn't in the company's price lists, one was entered in the 2008 Nürburgring 24 Hours. With regenerative braking and a 134bhp electric motor in tandem with a 3.3-litre twin-turbo V8, it proved that cutting-edge technology wasn't just for the big boys.

KEY CAR
APOLLO

BUILT	2005
ENGINE	4163cc, mid-mounted twin-turbo V8
POWER	650bhp @ 6500rpm
TORQUE	627lb ft @ 4000rpm
TOP SPEED	224mph
0–60MPH	3.1sec

INVICTA
A GREAT NAME REVIVED – BRIEFLY

The original Invicta sports car company manufactured cars between 1925 and 1950, at several locations and using parts from all sorts of companies. Offering such gems as the 3-Litre, S-Type and Black Prince, exclusivity was the name of the game; maybe too much so as the company could never operate on a scale large enough to make the project work.

When Invicta was relaunched in 2003, with the S1 as its only product, in some ways nothing had changed. The company was still very much a tiny player, and even though there was some heritage there – at least as far as the name was concerned – there was little in the way of brand awareness.

Despite the difficulty of launching a supercar into a market already full of well-known brands, Invicta was confident of its prospects. For those who wanted a civilised sportscar rather than something with which to tear up the road, there was a relatively tame 320bhp option – but for the power hungry there was also a 600bhp engine available. Whichever version was specified, power came from a 5-litre Ford-sourced V8, tuned by Ford's own Special Vehicle Team in the US; it could be hooked up to manual or automatic transmissions.

KEY CAR
S1

BUILT	2003
ENGINE	5-litre front-mounted supercharged V8
POWER	600bhp @ 4500rpm
TORQUE	575lb ft @ 4500rpm
TOP SPEED	200mph
0–60MPH	3.8sec

JAGUAR
GRACE, SPACE AND LOTS OF PACE

While its cars have always been premium products, Jaguar has always produced models offering superb performance at relatively affordable prices. Highlights have included the XK120–XK150 along with the fabulous E-Type, XJ-S and XKR. However, the definitive Jaguar supercar must be the XJ220, which first appeared in concept form in 1988.

Fitted with a V12 in the middle and four-wheel drive, the XJ220 was unveiled at the peak of a supercar boom, which is why the car proved an instant sell-out. Unfortunately, many who put their deposits down were speculators,

who then attempted to bail out as fast as possible when boom turned to bust. That's when things got very messy, with lawsuits flying all over the place.

Despite the legal wrangles, the XJ220 was still an amazing car. By the time it reached production it featured a twin-turbo V6 based on the same unit as the one fitted to the MG Metro 6R4. There was also rear-wheel drive only. In standard form the XJ220 could manage 211mph from its 542bhp powerplant, but for those who were seriously wealthy there was a Tom Walkinshaw Racing edition called the XJ220S. With its 680bhp V6 it could achieve 229mph – but very few were made.

KEY CAR
XJ220

BUILT	1992
ENGINE	3498cc, mid-mounted twin-turbo V6
POWER	542bhp @ 7000rpm
TORQUE	475lb ft @ 4500rpm
TOP SPEED	211mph
0–60MPH	3.6sec

KEATING
DAVID TAKES ON GOLIATH – AND WINS

When the Barabus was unveiled at the 2006 London motor show, everyone assumed it would sink without trace. Sure enough, it appeared to, because after that event the car disappeared from view. However, within a couple of years the Barabus would return as the Keating SKR and TKR; once again it was predicted the project would fail, but this time it didn't.

The SKR was a relatively tame supercar, its 6-litre GM-sourced LS2 V8 producing 400-656bhp, depending on the state of tune. This power was delivered to the rear wheels only, via a five-speed Porsche transaxle. However,

much more interesting was the TKR, visually the same as the SKR, and a true fire-breathing monster, thanks to a 7-litre twin-turbo LS7 V8, also from GM. Weighing just 1200kg or so, due to glassfibre or carbon-fibre bodywork, it was no surprise that the TKR was seriously fast.

To show just how fast its baby could travel, Keating took a TKR to California's Salt Lake flats to prove it was faster than a Bugatti Veyron. Sure enough, the car posted an unofficial top speed of 260.1mph – meaning this upstart Brit supercar had beaten the mighty Veyron, and all at a third of the cost.

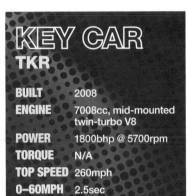

KEY CAR
TKR

BUILT	2008
ENGINE	7008cc, mid-mounted twin-turbo V8
POWER	1800bhp @ 5700rpm
TORQUE	N/A
TOP SPEED	260mph
0–60MPH	2.5sec

KOENIGSEGG
SWEDEN'S MOST EXCITING EXPORT

While older supercar manufacturers are well known, newcomers have to offer something very special if they want to get a look in. It's fair to say that Swedish company Koenigsegg doesn't have much history, but it builds one of the most powerful supercars ever, which makes up for any lack of heritage.

The thinking behind the Koenigsegg CC was that it should be the car to beat the McLaren F1. Brainchild of Christian von Koenigsegg, the first prototype was unveiled in 1995. However, it was five years before the first production car was unveiled, the wraps being taken off the CC at the Paris salon in October.

With its carbon-fibre monocoque structure and fully adjustable all-wishbone suspension, the Koenigsegg used key race-car technologies, but it was also a pioneer, with its paddle-shift transmission. The driver could also adjust the chassis, aerodynamic and braking settings from the cockpit – something which was very rare indeed.

Despite quickly gaining a reputation for high-quality, shatteringly fast cars, Koenigsegg didn't stop there. By 2004 there was the 806bhp CCR, but the ultimate model so far is the CCXR, capable of running on biofuel and developing up to 1018bhp.

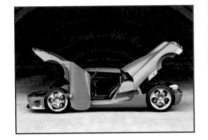

KEY CAR
CCXR

BUILT	2004
ENGINE	4700cc, mid-mounted twin-supercharged V8
POWER	1018bhp @ 6100rpm
TORQUE	782lb ft @ 6100rpm
TOP SPEED	249mph
0–60MPH	3.1sec

LAMBORGHINI
FROM TRACTORS TO SUPERCARS

Ferrari may have a higher profile because of its motorsport activities, but when it comes to extreme supercars, nobody can match Lamborghini's success. Just about every car it's ever made has been outrageous, from its first mid-engined effort – the Miura – to the latest Murciélago, with the insane V12-engined LM off-roader along the way.

Ferruccio Lamborghini began building supercars when his Ferrari proved unreliable and unrefined. Having made a fortune from building tractors and air conditioning systems, Lamborghini had plenty of money to spend on developing a supercar that was great to drive, looked sensational and was incredibly fast too. While his first efforts, the 350GT and 400GT, failed to set the world alight, the Miura did exactly that when it arrived in 1966. The world's first proper production mid-engined supercar, it created a template for the supercar of the future – and one which even the mighty Ferrari would have to follow.

When it was unveiled, Lamborghini reckoned it would build just a handful of Miuras and sell them for a very high price. In the event, Lamborghini couldn't

make them quickly enough. The P400 was the first Miura, packing a 350bhp V12, with the P400S of 1968 upping that to 370bhp. Best of the lot though was the Miura SV of 1971, with its 385bhp giving a 172mph top speed.

While the Miura had been striking and beautiful, the Countach which followed was nothing less than brutal. ▶

KEY CAR
MIURA SV

BUILT	1971
ENGINE	3929cc, mid-mounted V12
POWER	370bhp @ 7700rpm
TORQUE	286lb ft @ 5500rpm
TOP SPEED	172mph
0–60MPH	6.7sec

Unveiled in concept form at the 1971 Geneva motor show, this ludicrously low and wide wedge was fitted with the most outrageous door design ever devised. It was 1974 before the first Countach was delivered to its owner though; by now some changes to the body had been made to reduce overheating problems, but the car hadn't lost any of its looks.

Over the next 15 years or so the Countach developed, gaining a 5-litre engine in place of the original 4-litre unit. This then grew to 5.2 litres, fuel injection replaced the six carburettors and a redesigned cylinder head arrived in 1985, with four valves for each cylinder. However, the ultimate Countach was the 173mph Anniversary of 1988, to commemorate 25 years of Lamborghini. More usable than earlier versions of the car, this was also the ugliest Countach by miles, thanks to a hideous body kit.

By 1990 the Countach was dead, replaced by the Diablo, which used the same V12 but now displacing 5.7 litres and featuring electronic multi-point fuel injection to give 492bhp. Once more there was development of the car: the four-wheel drive VT arrived in 1993, and from 1995 this was also offered in Roadster form. The 595bhp SE30 of 1994 celebrated three decades of Lamborghini, but the turning point came with the launch of the Diablo 6.0 in 1999, a year after Audi bought Lamborghini. With styling revisions, redesigned wheels, an overhauled interior and a 5992cc engine, this was the ultimate production Diablo – although even this would appear tame compared with its replacement...

When the Murciélago arrived in 2001, even the Diablo that preceded it was put in the shade. Here was a 6.2-litre V12 beast with four-wheel drive as standard, which could supposedly manage 210mph; the Roadster edition that appeared in 2004 was claimed to be just as fast. After that however, things started to ▶

KEY CAR
DIABLO SV

BUILT	1995
ENGINE	5992cc, mid-mounted V12
POWER	550bhp @ 7100rpm
TORQUE	457lb ft @ 5500rpm
TOP SPEED	208mph
0–60MPH	4.0sec

get really interesting in 2006 when the 630bhp 6.5-litre Murciélago LP640 arrived, but the ultimate version is the LP670-4 SV, which was launched in 2009. Its 661bhp V12 engine was able to take the car to 213mph, and this was designed to be the very last Murciélago before an all-new car arrived.

KEY CAR
MURCIELAGO LP-670 SV

BUILT	2009
ENGINE	6496cc, mid-mounted V12
POWER	661bhp @ 8000rpm
TORQUE	487lb ft @ 6500rpm
TOP SPEED	213mph
0–60MPH	2.9sec

LEXUS
THE FIRST JAPANESE HYPERCAR

Just a few years ago, the thought of a Lexus getting into these pages would have been laughable. Better known for its luxury saloons, which offer little in the way of driver enjoyment, Lexus first displayed its LF-A supercar concept at the 2005 Detroit motor show. Over the next few years, revised concepts were shown, resulting in a roadster edition being unveiled at the 2008 Detroit motor show.

Like the Bugatti Veyron, testing of the LF-A seemed to go on forever, until at last a production car was unveiled in October 2009, now known as the LFA. Powered by a naturally aspirated V10,

which was built especially for the car, there was a mouth-watering 552bhp on tap. When this was combined with a carbon-fibre bodyshell to give a 1480kg kerb weight, the Lexus was capable of cracking 200mph.

Bearing in mind the £336,000 price tag at launch, there was clearly a limited number of buyers for this Japanese supercar, but to guarantee rarity, it was decided at the start to produce only 500 cars. Whether or not anything from Japan will ever beat the LFA remains to be seen; it's not very likely that Lexus ever made any money on the project.

KEY CAR
LFA

BUILT	2010
ENGINE	4805cc, front-mounted V10
POWER	552bhp @ 8700rpm
TORQUE	480lb ft @ 6800rpm
TOP SPEED	202mph
0–60MPH	3.7sec

LOTEC
SOMETHING VERY SPECIAL FROM GERMANY

Kurt Lotterschmid's first creation, the C1000 of 1992, didn't have much of an impact on the supercar world. Fitted with an 854bhp road-legal version of the Sauber C9 Le Mans car's twin-turbo Mercedes V8, the car was distinctive, beautifully built and shatteringly fast. The C1000 was so good, that before Lotterschmid could put it into production, it was snapped up by a wealthy sheikh for his personal use.

Unfortunately it seems Lotterschmid's second car, the 2004 Sirius, is likely also to remain in the shadows, as the company isn't able to produce any more than five cars each year – and they may not even be producing that many.

Still, Lotec is making sure that each Sirius counts, because even basic models have 850bhp on tap and the promise of well over 200mph; choose the longer final drive and higher turbo boost pressures (there are two turbos strapped to the Mercedes V12) and there's an unbelievable 1200bhp on offer. When you combine that with a kerb weight of 1390kg, some quite impressive performance figures are guaranteed, while the ride and handling are taken care of with a chassis full of racing tricks. And all at half the price of a Veyron…

KEY CAR
SIRIUS

BUILT	2004
ENGINE	5987cc, mid-mounted V12
POWER	1200bhp @ 6300rpm
TORQUE	974lb ft @ 3400rpm
TOP SPEED	242mph
0–60MPH	3.8sec

MASERATI
ITALY'S FORGOTTEN SUPERCAR BUILDER

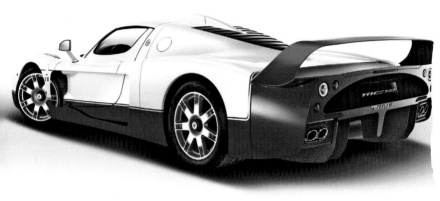

Despite an incredible racing heritage, Maserati has always been something of a forgotten hero. Not as bright and brash as its Italian rivals, Ferrari and Lamborghini, for many years Maserati was a bit lost in the woods, as it passed from one owner to another. Despite this, the Italian marque has come up with a series of great V8-engined cars, including the Ghibli, Bora and GranTurismo.

However, without doubt the high point of Maserati's portfolio was its Ferrari Enzo-based MC12, which arrived in 2005. Even more expensive and exclusive than the Enzo, the MC12 wasn't quite as fast – but a 205mph top speed was probably enough

for most buyers. Such speed was possible due to a six-litre V12 based on the Enzo's powerplant, while weight was kept to a minimum with carbon-fibre construction.

The car came about because, after a 37-year break in motorsport, Maserati decided to take part in the Le Mans 24 Hours. To compete in the GT class, the company would have to make 25 road-going versions of its race car available. In the end, 25 were made in 2004, with another run of 25 produced the following year. Each one weighed just 1335kg, so it's no wonder the MC12 could get from 0 to 124mph (200kmh) in just six seconds.

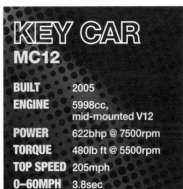

KEY CAR
MC12

BUILT	2005
ENGINE	5998cc, mid-mounted V12
POWER	622bhp @ 7500rpm
TORQUE	480lb ft @ 5500rpm
TOP SPEED	205mph
0–60MPH	3.8sec

McLAREN
RACE CAR KNOW-HOW FOR THE ROAD

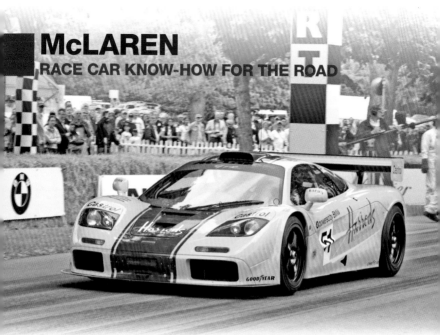

We'll never see anything like it again, so it's a shame that just 60 or so road-going F1s were built, along with another 40 or so racers. Designed to be the ultimate supercar, McLaren spared no expense in the development and construction of the F1, from its carbon composite monocoque to its all-alloy V12 bought in from BMW Motorsport.

While the bodyshell and powerplant were hugely expensive, so too was the transmission, which used Formula One ideas. Just the rear wheels were driven, with power being transmitted via a small carbon clutch and aluminium flywheel, ensuring a lightning-fast response.

There was as little technology as possible to harm the driving experience, which is why there was no power steering, no brake servo and no traction control. The result was a car that offered the most amazing driving experience imaginable – so it's a shame that few would ever get the chance to enjoy it.

After the F1's demise, McLaren teamed up with Mercedes to produce the SLR, which was never especially well admired, despite its massive price tag. Mercedes continued alone with the SLR's successor, the SLS, leaving McLaren to come up with the MP12-4C in 2009. Definitely another hugely desirable supercar, but it was no F1…

KEY CAR
F1

BUILT	1994
ENGINE	6064cc, mid-mounted V12
POWER	627bhp @ 7000rpm
TORQUE	479lb ft @ 4000rpm
TOP SPEED	240mph
0–60MPH	3.6sec

MERCEDES
WORLD'S OLDEST CAR MAKER SHOWS HOW IT'S DONE

The oldest car maker in the world, Mercedes-Benz has also produced some of the most powerful cars, but it has never followed the classic mid-engined supercar market like most of the other manufacturers in this book. Don't let that fool you though; from its early days – before anybody else among these pages even existed – Mercedes has produced astonishingly fast machines. As early as 1909 the 21½-litre Blitzen Benz had secured the land speed record at 131mph; a year later it had pushed this up to nearly 142mph.

Mercedes continued to push the limits, and its 225bhp SSK of 1928 was capable of 126mph when most others struggled beyond

50mph. Further masterpieces followed, such as the 500K and 540K, the latter featuring a 180bhp supercharged 5.4-litre straight-eight.

After the Second World War, Mercedes continued to produce some incredible designs, including the 300SL 'Gullwing'. While it's the road cars that have become legends, these were based on a racer that was created to bring Mercedes back to motorsport, after the war had ended. The 300SL

wasn't that advanced technically, but it did feature mechanical fuel injection. More impressive were its aerodynamics and lightweight construction, plus the performance and power on offer – a 140mph top speed in 1954 was seriously impressive.

As time progressed, Mercedes introduced steadily more powerful cars; ▶

KEY CAR
300SL

BUILT	1954
ENGINE	2996cc, front-mounted straight-six
POWER	240bhp @ 6100rpm
TORQUE	217lb ft @ 4800rpm
TOP SPEED	140mph
0–60MPH	8.8sec

fast and capable coupés, convertibles and luxury saloons were offered with huge power outputs and high top speeds. The 300SEL 6.3 of 1968 was the turning point as this was the first model that was in effect a factory hot-rod. Using the S-Class model as its basis, the 6.3-litre V8 of the massive 600 limousine was shoehorned under the bonnet – and 6526 were then sold, proving that people wanted such a fast luxury cruiser.

Next came the 450SEL 6.9 of 1974; not much more than the newer S-Class with a bigger V8, it proved even more popular, with 7380 produced. By the 1980s though, Mercedes had moved into overdrive with hot editions of its cars, often wearing AMG badges. At this point AMG was separate to Mercedes, but in time it would become a part of the company. That's when the floodgates really opened, with massively powerful versions of pretty much every Mercedes model line being introduced. Craziest of the lot was the 612bhp CLK-GTR of 1999, limited to just 35 or so road and race cars; easier to get hold of was the SLR McLaren of 2003 and its successor the SLS of 2010.

KEY CAR
SLR McLAREN

BUILT	2003
ENGINE	5439cc front-mounted supercharged V8
POWER	626bhp @ 6500rpm
TORQUE	575lb ft @ 3250rpm
TOP SPEED	206mph
0–60MPH	3.8sec

NOBLE
A TINY BRITISH MARQUE STEPS UP A GEAR

Set up by Lee Noble in 1999, Noble Automotive's mission was to create brilliant driver's cars without charging silly prices. Providing an alternative to Lotus was a plan that worked, with the company's M12 and M400 proving very popular. Offering up to 425bhp from its mid-mounted turbocharged Ford Duratec V6, the M400 offered serious thrills with decent reliability at a relatively affordable price.

By 2006 though Noble had sold his company, and although at first he remained involved, he walked away in 2008. That was around the time the M12 project was being sold to 1G

Racing in the US, where it would go into production as the Rossion Q1. By 2009 though, Noble Automotive would unveil a new car and Lee Noble would unveil a new company – Fenix Automotive.

When Noble relaunched in 2009, it had taken a big leap forward, as now on offer there was a supercar rather than a mere sportscar. It was the M600, powered by a mid-mounted 4.4-litre V8 taken from the Volvo parts bin, with two turbochargers bolted on to give a rather fruity 650bhp. Noble made a big deal of the M600's exclusivity, but with a £200,000 price tag, the car was never going to be a big seller…

KEY CAR
M600

BUILT	2010
ENGINE	4439cc, mid-mounted twin-turbo V8
POWER	650bhp @ 6800rpm
TORQUE	604lb ft @ 3800rpm
TOP SPEED	225mph
0–60MPH	3.0sec

M600 GB

PAGANI
PROOF THAT SIZE DOESN'T MATTER

Horacio Pagani came from nowhere in 1999, to launch his own supercar company – and where others have failed, this Italian company has thrived. It helped that Pagani already had links with Ferrari and Lamborghini, for whom he'd done specialist composite work on their lightweight bodyshells; such experience was essential for the Zonda, named after a wind from the Andes.

The first Zonda, the C12, was powered by a 5987cc Mercedes V12; just five were made before a 7010cc AMG-tuned V12 was used instead. In the process the car became known as the C12S; this would also be the first Zonda to be offered in open-topped form. After just 15 copies of the C12S had been produced, the C12S 7.3 appeared in 2002, now with 547bhp.

The development would continue though, with the 594bhp Zonda F being unveiled in 2005 and the track-focused Zonda R Clubsport making its appearance in 2007. However, of more interest to collectors is the Zonda Cinque, offered as a coupé and convertible from 2009. As the name suggests, just five examples of each bodystyle were built, priced at around $1m apiece. A lot of cash undoubtedly, but the Cinque was also the most powerful road-going Zonda ever built, with a 678bhp 7.3-litre V12.

KEY CAR
ZONDA CINQUE

BUILT	2009
ENGINE	7291cc, V12
POWER	678bhp @ 6500rpm
TORQUE	575lb ft @ 4200rpm
TOP SPEED	217mph
0–60MPH	3.4sec

PORSCHE
RACE CAR ENGINEERING FOR THE ROAD

From its earliest days, Porsche has built driving machines for the enthusiast. The first 356s were lightweight and agile, so even though they had little in the way of power, they were still great to drive. First seen in 1948, the original 356 used plenty of VW Beetle parts to keep manufacturing costs down, but the design was swiftly refined and over the next 15

years a line of 356s followed, including open-topped and more powerful versions.

The turning point for Porsche came in 1963 when the company unveiled its 901. Quickly renamed 911 after Peugeot (who name all their cars with three numbers, always with a 0 in the middle) objected, this rear-engined sportscar defined Porsche – and the usable supercar.

BB·PW 287

Although the first 911s weren't very powerful – they produced just 128bhp – they were fast if somewhat tricky to drive on the limit due to the engine being mounted at the back. It wasn't long though before more powerful engines became available; by 1965 there was 158bhp on tap, boosted to 178bhp in 1969.

KEY CAR
959

BUILT	1986
ENGINE	2851cc, rear-mounted turbocharged flat-six
POWER	450bhp @ 6500rpm
TORQUE	370lb ft @ 5500rpm
TOP SPEED	197mph
0–60MPH	3.6sec

In the early 1970s there were several iconic 911s such as the Carrera RS 2.7, but a milestone was the arrival of the Turbo in 1974, complete with whale-tail spoiler. Shatteringly fast, the car was noted for its high price, massive acceleration, tricky handling and ludicrous turbo lag. In the following years the Turbo was refined by adding intercoolers, better engine management systems and constantly redesigned parts for greater efficiency and performance.

The next turning point came when the 964-Series was launched in 1989. For the first time ever, the 911 was offered with four-wheel drive, although a rear-wheel-drive version was still available. The car was also more aerodynamic than before, while the engine grew from 3.2 litres to 3.6, resulting in a jump from 231bhp to 247bhp.

While the 964 was a welcome step forward for the 911 in terms of usability, the 993 that replaced it in 1993 was an even greater leap. The 993 was also the final air-cooled 911 before the water-cooled 996 of 1998. While the standard 993 was an impressive car, the Turbo edition that arrived in 1995 was even better, as it now had a 408bhp twin-turbo flat-six, with standard four-wheel drive to help keep the car going in the right direction.

Long before the 996 appeared, Porsche had made a confusing range of 911 cars, but this new model took things even further.

BUILT	2008
ENGINE	3600cc, rear-mounted turbocharged flat-six
POWER	523bhp @ 6500rpm
TORQUE	502lb ft @ 2200rpm
TOP SPEED	204mph
0–60MPH	3.7sec

During a seven-year production run there was a huge variety of names, including the GT2, GT3, Turbo, Carrera 4 and more. This is a plan that Porsche stuck with when it introduced the next-generation 911 in 2005. Named the 997, there were once again a confusing number of models including the GT3 RS and the truly monstrous GT2, which ▶

featured a 523bhp twin-turbo 3.6-litre flat-six. As a result, it was the first street-legal production 911 to officially be able to exceed 200mph; its top speed was 204mph.

As well as the 911, Porsche has built plenty more performance cars, such as the V8-engined 928, the four-cylinder 944 and the ultra-rare 959. The 959 was introduced in 1986 as a truly cutting-edge road and race car; just 337 were built, with a 444bhp twin-turbo 2.85-litre flat-six and the world's most advanced four-wheel drive system.

As a result of its rarity, the 959 is

among the most sought after of all the Porsches – much like the Carrera GT of 2004. Fitted with a 5.7-litre V10 in the middle, this is the most advanced Porsche yet due to its carbon-fibre construction, carbon ceramic brakes and race-car design for all the systems including the brakes and suspension.

KEY CAR
CARRERA GT

BUILT	2004
ENGINE	5733cc, mid-mounted V10
POWER	612bhp @ 8000rpm
TORQUE	435lb ft @ 5750rpm
TOP SPEED	205mph
0–60MPH	3.3sec

SALEEN
THE AMERICAN LAMBORGHINI-BEATER

There haven't been many supercars to come from America, but perhaps the most desirable is this one: the Saleen S7. Beautifully designed and built, the S7 is also one of the few road-going cars that gets close to cracking the 250mph barrier.

Engineered in the UK, the Saleen is named after its founder Steve Saleen, who made his name tuning Mustangs for racing; it was just a matter of time before he made his own fully fledged supercar. Whereas most hypercars feature cutting-edge technology, the S7 is relatively low-tech in that there's a glassfibre and carbon-fibre bodyshell over a tubular steel spaceframe, which houses a pushrod V8.

The first cars, built in 2000, were fitted with a normally aspirated engine, capable of developing just 500bhp. Clearly the car was in danger of being outclassed by fully laden milk floats, which is why a twin-turbo V8 was fitted from 2005. Tuned to give 750bhp, the S7's top speed jumped from a claimed 210mph to a supposed 248mph. However, with a background in preparing competition cars, Saleen also offered race-prepared S7s from the start. Run exclusively by private racing drivers, the S7 has gone on to become the most successful road-going supercar-based racer ever.

KEY CAR
S7

BUILT	2005
ENGINE	6998cc, mid-mounted twin-turbo V8
POWER	750bhp @ 6300rpm
TORQUE	700lb ft @ 4800rpm
TOP SPEED	248mph
0–60MPH	2.8sec

SHELBY
AMERICAN KNOW-HOW THAT BEAT THE VEYRON

While Bugatti's Veyron grabs all the headlines about being the world's fastest car, America's SSC Ultimate Aero TT is officially faster. While the Veyron has been timed at a mere 252mph, the Ultimate Aero TT is capable of 257mph, and there's the promise of more – 287mph with the right gearing.

The Aero project started out in 2006, using a 6-litre supercharged V8, based on the engine more usually seen in the Corvette. Boosted to give 1062bhp at 6600rpm, this engine was developed further for its fitment to the Ultimate Aero. The capacity was increased to 6.34 litres, while the supercharger's boost pressure

was also increased to boost power to 1147bhp at 6950rpm.

Not happy to stick with such a weedy engine, for 2007 Shelby Supercars developed a twin-turbo 6.35-litre V8, which could produce 1183bhp. However, the car's equipment level was also increased, along with its weight, which is why for 2008 an all-new engine was developed. Supposedly already capable of taking the Ultimate Aero TT to 267mph, power was boosted yet again for 2009, to an incredible 1287bhp – enough to take the car to a theoretical top speed of 287mph. That was 35mph more than a Bugatti Veyron…

KEY CAR
ULTIMATE AERO TT

BUILT	2007
ENGINE	6342cc, V8
POWER	1183bhp @ 6950rpm
TORQUE	1094lb ft @ 6150rpm
TOP SPEED	257mph
0–60MPH	2.8sec

SPYKER
A TOUCH OF DUTCH COURAGE

The original Spyker car company (then Spijker) was set up in 1880 as a Dutch coachbuilder; from 1899 it also made cars, which it produced until it went bust in 1926. In 1999, the name was brought back by a new Dutch company, to build some of the most ornate supercars ever devised.

The first car unveiled by the revived Spyker was the C8 Spyder in 2000, which featured one of the most lavish car interiors ever seen. Within a year there was a coupé edition named the Laviolette, then in 2002 came the C8 Double 12, to go with a Le Mans endurance racer of the same name.

The development continued, with a twin-turbo C8 arriving in 2003, called the Spyder T. Until recently, all modern Spykers featured an Audi 4.2-litre V8, but in 2005 came the C12 LaTurbie, with a 6-litre Audi W12 in the middle.

However, by 2009 Spyker's standard production cars still all had no more than eight cylinders – although the seriously rich could order a $650,000 C12 Zagato if they wanted to. With the same 6-litre W12 that had been seen in the LaTurbie, the car promised all the speed with even more glamour, thanks to a tie up with Italian styling house Zagato.

KEY CAR
C12 ZAGATO

BUILT	2009
ENGINE	5998cc mid-mounted W12
POWER	500bhp
TORQUE	450lb ft
TOP SPEED	195mph
0–60MPH	3.8sec

ULTIMA
PROOF THAT TOO MUCH IS NOT ENOUGH

Ultima GTR

Years before Lee Noble set up Noble Automotive, he started Noble Motorsport to build the Ultima. That was in 1983, when the engine and gearbox were taken from a Renault 30 – although it wasn't long before the car was redesigned to take a Ford Essex V6 engine. With Noble's first customer (Ted Marlow) a keen racer – as was Noble himself – it wouldn't be long before the Ultima was developed to take V8 power.

Sure enough, by the late 1980s Marlow's Ultima came with a Chevrolet 6.2-litre V8 and Noble had redesigned the car to come up with the Mk3. By 1992 Noble had walked away from the project, selling it to Marlow who launched a Spyder edition in 1993. But the real high point came in 1999 with the unveiling of the GTR, which would push Ultima into the limelight as it broke one speed record after another.

Offered in kit form, or as a finished car, the GTR could be fitted with a Chevrolet V8 offering up to 1000bhp. This combined with a kerb weight of just 990kg was guaranteed to give shattering performance. Indeed, pitched against a McLaren F1 and Bugatti Veyron, the GTR proved quickest. Which is probably fast enough for most.

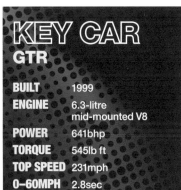

KEY CAR
GTR

BUILT	1999
ENGINE	6.3-litre mid-mounted V8
POWER	641bhp
TORQUE	545lb ft
TOP SPEED	231mph
0–60MPH	2.8sec

VECTOR

THE SUPERCAR THAT THOUGHT IT WAS AN AIRCRAFT

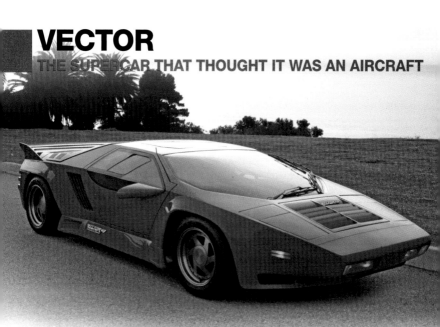

As long ago as 1977 the Vector Aeromotive W2 burst onto the supercar scene. Company founder Gerry Wiegert was obsessed with aeronautical technology and reckoned there was a place for it in a road car. By the time the W8 arrived in 1991, this obsession with aircraft-grade construction came with a $450,000 price tag, which is why customers were scarce.

At the heart of the W8 was a finely designed six-litre all-alloy V8 with forged aluminium pistons, a forged crankshaft and stainless steel valves. There were two turbochargers and electronic direct port fuel injection to produce 625bhp at 5700rpm and 630lb ft of torque at 4900rpm; with this

the W8 was supposed to be capable of topping 200mph while making the 0–60mph dash in barely four seconds.

Despite its cost, 14 W8s were bought before the car was followed by the Avtech WX-3 in 1992. If the price tag attached to the earlier car had seemed a bit extreme, the $765,000 cost of the new car was even more outrageous. Unsurprisingly, there were no takers for the car and as a result Vector Aeromotive was taken over by Mega Tech, the Indonesian company which also owned Lamborghini. The M12 that resulted featured a Lamborghini V12, but it's doubtful that any were sold.

KEY CAR
W8

BUILT	1991
ENGINE	5973cc, mid-mounted twin-turbo V8
POWER	625bhp @ 5700rpm
TORQUE	630lb ft @ 4900rpm
TOP SPEED	218mph
0–60MPH	4.2sec

YAMAHA

In the world of the supercar, when you hear the words 'race car for the road' then it is usually just sales speak, but in the case of Yamaha it was truly deserved. So it's a shame that the OX99-11 never actually went on sale as it's one of the few cars that could have given the Mclaren F1 a run for its money.

The OX99-11 appeared in 1992, with a 420bhp 3.5-litre V12 engine fitted in the middle; this was a less-powerful version of the engine fitted to the Brabhams and Jordans of the early 1990s. Also, the chassis was a carbon-fibre honeycomb monocoque,

so the OX99-11 really did use cutting-edge F1 technology.

If you added a proper bodyshell, air-conditioning, an all-synchromesh gearbox and exhaust catalysts to a Formula One car then this would be the result. However, after all this ultra-modern technology, there was one throwback to another era, and that was the hand-beaten alloy panelling, chosen instead of carbon-fibre to give the right impression of exclusivity. The price was an eye-watering $1m, but where else could you get anything like it? Just three were built before the project was abandoned.

KEY CAR
OX99-11

BUILT	1992
ENGINE	3498cc, V12
POWER	420bhp @ 10,000rpm
TORQUE	N/A
TOP SPEED	219mph
0–60MPH	3.1sec

ZENVO

AND NOW – THE SUPERCAR FROM DENMARK

Take a look at the map of supercar makers and you'll see that there aren't very many in Denmark, but it's Jesper Jensen's mission to change all that, with his Zenvo ST1 hypercar. As this book was being written the ST1 had still to be seen in the metal (well, carbon-fibre actually), so any predictions about its performance were yet to be proved – but that didn't make it any less exciting.

At the heart of the ST1 is a 7-litre V8 that is both supercharged and turbocharged. The US-built engine can run on either petrol or E85 bio-ethanol, and give up to 1104bhp.

Thanks to a kerb weight of just 1376kg, that's enough to give a power-to-weight ratio of over 800bhp per tonne – which results in a very tasty 233mph top speed. Zenvo claims it could be even higher, but an electronic limiter stops the fun at that point – spoilsports.

Time will tell whether or not the Zenvo will ever see the light of day, but with a £770,000 price tag it's unlikely that the queue will be very long. Still, as Zenvo plans to build no more than 15 examples of the ST1 from the outset, its targets aren't especially ambitious.

KEY CAR
ST1

BUILT	2010
ENGINE	7-litre mid-mounted twin-turbo V8
POWER	1104bhp @ 6900rpm
TORQUE	1055lb ft @ 4500rpm
TOP SPEED	233mph
0–60MPH	3.0sec

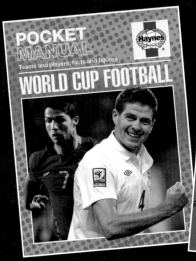
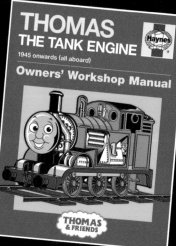